Favorite Pets

Written by Cathy Jones
Reading consultants: Christopher Collier and Alan Howe, Bath Spa University, UK

First published by Parragon in 2009
Parragon
Queen Street House
4 Queen Street
Bath BA1 1HE, UK

ISBN 978-1-4075-8784-4

Printed in China

Favorite Pets

Bath · New York · Singapore · Hong Kong · Cologne · Delhi · Melbourne

Contents

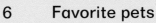

cheese

Favorite pets

A pet is a **domesticated** animal that you keep for company. Most pets share your home, where you can care for them. All kinds of different animals can be kept as pets.

The most popular pets are cats, dogs, rabbits, mice, hamsters, fish, and birds.

All pets need somewhere to sleep, food, water, exercise, and care.

Many pets are small, furry **mammals** with sharp teeth and claws. Be gentle when you hold them so that they are not scared.

DiscoveryFact™

The ancient Egyptians kept cats to hunt mice and rats in the home.

Choosing your pet

Choosing the right pet for you can be tricky. Think about how much time you can spend with it. How much space it will need? How quiet or noisy is your home?

goldfish

✔ **Birds** are beautiful pets.
✘ But they can be noisy.

✔ **Cats** are very calm and clean.
✘ But they can scratch the furniture.

✔ **Dogs** are very loyal and love to play.
✘ But they need space to run around.

✔ **Fish** are great to watch.
✘ But fish tanks are difficult to clean.

✔ **Hamsters** are easy to care for.
✘ But they run around at night.

✔ **Mice** are very friendly.
✘ But they can get free easily.

✔ **Rabbits** are very clean animals.
✘ But they are easily scared.

DiscoveryFact™

Pets are good for you. They make you feel happy and calm. Doctors say that people who own pets don't get sick as much.

Getting to know your pet

When you bring your pet home, you will need to look after it. Find it a special place to sleep. Give it the right food, fresh water, and plenty of exercise.

Approach your pet quietly so that it is not scared. Let it sniff and explore you until it feels calm.

A small pet can be picked up gently. Put your hand under its belly just below the front legs. Support the back legs with your other hand.

You can train cats and rabbits to use a **litter box**. Dogs need to go outside.

Clean out your pet's cage regularly. A dirty cage can make your pet sick. Keep the cage away from cold, windy places or hot, sunny places.

DiscoveryFact™

Stick insects can live for about 1 year.
Mice can live for about 2 years.
Hamsters can live for about 3 years.
Rats can live for about 4 years.
Guinea pigs can live for about 5 years.
Rabbits can live for about 10 years.

Dogs

There are about 200 different **breeds**, or types, of dog to choose from. All the dog breeds we have today are related to the gray wolf.

dog

Find a basket, blanket, or cushion where your dog can sleep. It will like to have its own toys and old blankets that smell familiar.

dog food

Give your dog moist, meaty dog food, crunchy, dry dog food and water to drink.

DiscoveryFact™

Dogs can't sweat to keep cool like we do. Instead, they pant with their tongues hanging out. Don't leave your dog in a hot place!

Dogs mark their **territory** by peeing to leave a **scent**.

Dogs love to run and play. Take your dog for a walk at least once a day.

Cats

Like wild cats, such as tigers, pet cats hunt on their own. They go out and roam, marking their territory with scent. This warns other cats not to take over their space.

Give your cat a basket or pillow to sleep on. A cat leaves a scent on favorite places by rubbing its face against them.

cat

Give your cat moist cat food, dry food, and water to drink. Cats need to eat small amounts throughout the day.

Brush your cat to get rid of loose fur. This will help stop it from getting **hair balls**.

Dangle a piece of string or a toy when your cat is feeling playful. It will help your pet learn to chase and pounce.

DiscoveryFact™

When they are not hunting, cats spend most of their time napping—about 16 hours a day!

Rabbits and guinea pigs

Rabbits and guinea pigs are quiet animals, but your pet may be lonely by itself. A pet rabbit will get along well with other rabbits. A pet guinea pig will get along well with other guinea pigs.

Rabbits and guinea pigs can live indoors or outdoors. They will need a **hutch** with a shaded place to eat and sleep. They also need a warm, dark place with fresh straw to sleep in.

grass

hamster

litter box

medicine

guinea pig

leaves

whiskers   exercise

gerbil

wood shavings

hutch

Indian stick insect

Rabbits and guinea pigs are **herbivores**. They eat grass, leaves, fruit, and vegetables, and they drink water.

Your pet will spend a lot of time grooming itself. You can help by brushing your pet's fur with a special brush.

17

Mice and rats

Mice and rats are **rodents**. In the wild, they live in large family groups. They will enjoy playing with you if you are gentle.

Your pet mouse or rat will need a large, strong wire cage. Line the cage with straw or cat litter. Add a small cardboard box and paper towels for your pet to make its nest.

Rats are **omnivores**. They eat almost anything—except cheese, which is bad for them.

Give your pet mouse cereal grains, seeds, chunks of fruit, and vegetables, and water to drink twice a day.

Mice and rats can't see very well but they have good senses of smell, taste, and hearing. Whiskers help them feel their way in burrows.

Your pet will need plenty of exercise, so put an exercise wheel in the cage.

Hamsters and gerbils

Hamsters and gerbils are also rodents.
They are small, furry, and easy to hold.

Line a wire cage with
paper and wood shavings
for your pet to nest in.
It will love cardboard or
plastic tubes to run in.

Hamsters have
large cheeks
like sacks,
where they
store food to
eat later.

Hamsters are omnivores. They eat insects, worms, seeds, cereal, fruit, and vegetables.

Gerbils are herbivores. They eat nuts, seeds, oats, crunchy vegetables, and fruit.

Hamsters are happy to be on their own. Gerbils get lonely, so it is best to have two gerbils.

Other pets

There are many other pets. Unusual ones can be fun if you choose them carefully.

Goldfish

You may not be able to cuddle a goldfish, but they are fun to watch. Your pet will soon see you coming at feeding time.

Don't pick up a gecko by its tail, or it may break off. A gecko sheds its tail to get free. The tail grows back in about six months.

Leopard Gecko
A leopard gecko is a **reptile**. It looks like a mini-dinosaur!

Parakeet
Parakeets are busy, talkative pets. They can even copy words you say or make the sound of the doorbell ringing.

Indian stick insect
A stick insect is interesting—if you can find it! It is **camouflaged** so it can hide from **predators**.

The veterinarian

If your pet is ill, you will need to take it to the **veterinarian**. Your pet may be sick if it:

- is not eating
- constantly scratches itself
- is losing its fur
- has crusty eyes
- has runny poop

Find a safe basket or box with air holes in it to carry your pet. Put in a favorite toy or blanket. Talk to your pet.

The veterinarian will check your pet and tell you what you need to do to make it better.

Claws may need to be clipped.

Teeth may need to be cleaned.

Your pet might need medicine.

Quiz

Now try this quiz!

All the answers can be found in this book.

What pet did the ancient Egyptians
keep to hunt mice and rats in the home?

(a) Cats
(b) Dogs
(c) Goldfish

How long can rabbits live for?

(a) About 1 year
(b) About 5 years
(c) About 10 years

How many breeds of dog are there?

(a) About 20
(b) About 100
(c) About 200

How do cats like to hunt?

(a) In packs
(b) On their own
(c) In pairs

What food is bad for rats?

(a) Nuts
(b) Meat
(c) Cheese

What do hamsters store in their cheeks?

(a) Food
(b) Water
(c) Wood shavings

Glossary

Breed   A group of similar animals that are descended from the same ancestors.

Camouflage   Animal colors and markings that blend in with the animal's background.

Domesticated   Living alongside people.

Hair ball   Ball of fur that collects in an animal's stomach as it grooms itself.

Herbivore   An animal that eats plants.

Hutch   A wooden cage, usually raised off the ground.

Litter box   An indoor toilet for pets, usually a plastic tray lined with pellets.

Mammal   A warm-blooded animal with hairy or furry skin that gives birth to live young.

Omnivore   An animal that eats meat and plants.

Predator   An animal that hunts another animal for food.

Reptile   A cold-blooded, scaly-skinned animal that lays eggs.

Rodent   A family of animals that includes mice, rats, guinea pigs, hamsters, and gerbils.

Scent   The smell that an animal makes so that it can mark its territory.

Territory   The area that an animal guards, where it lives and finds food.

Veterinarian   An animal doctor.

Index

Acknowledgments

t=top, c=center, b=bottom, r=right, l=left

Front cover: Getty Images/Pat Powers and Cherryl Schafer
Back cover: l Getty Images/American Images Inc, r Getty Images/GK Hart/Vikki Hart

1 Getty Images/GK Hart/Vikki Hart, 2 dreamstime.com/Enika,
3 Getty Images/American Images Inc, 4 istockphoto/Matt Staples,
5tl istockphoto/Andrea Krause, 5bl Dreamstime.com/Cardiae,
5br Getty Images/GK Hart/Vikki Hart, 6-7 istockphoto/Pamspix,
6 istockphoto/ Jonny Kristoffersson, 7t istockphoto/ Erik Hougaard,
7c Getty Images/Kenneth Garrett, 8-9 Getty Images/Muriel de Seze,
9 istockphoto/Alex Gumerov, 10-11 Getty Images/Ariel Skelley,
11t istockphoto/Rosemarie Gearhart, 11cr Getty Images/Jane Burton,
11cl istockphoto/ andres balcazar, 12-13 istockphoto/Eric Isselée,
12 dreamstime.com/davisflowerlady, 13tl istockphoto/ Sergey Siz`kov,
13 cr istockphoto/Andrea Krause, 13 cl istockphoto/winhorse,
13 br istockphoto/sonyae, 14 Getty Images/ Sven Hagolani,
14l istockphoto/Jennifer Sheets, 15 tl Melinda Fawver,
15 cl istockphoto/Gregory Albertini, 15br Getty Images/GK Hart/Vikki
Hart, 16-17 istockphoto/Cynoclub, 16 cl istockphoto/Rachel Giles,
17 tr dreamstime.com/Enika, 17 cr Getty Images/
Steve Teague, 18-19 istockphoto/Lone Elisa Plougmann,
18 tl istockphoto/Dmitry Maslov, 18 bl istockphoto/Vasyl Helevachuk,
18br Getty Images/Steve Gorton, 19 tr Getty Images/Martin Harvey,
19 Getty Images/Image Source, 20-21 istockphoto/Matt Staples,
20tl dreamstime.com/Cardiae, 20 br Getty Images/Jane Burton,
21 b dreamstime.com/alexkalashnikov, 22 Getty Images/GK Hart/
Vikki Hart, 23 tr istockphoto/Lee Ingram, 23 cl Getty Images/ Gerold
& Cynthia Merker, 23 b istockphoto/ Nancy Nehring, 24 istockphoto/
Willie B. Thomas, 25 t Getty Images/ John Wood Photography,
25 tl dreamstime.com/ Ankevanwyk, 25 cl istockphoto/Savany,
25 bl istockphoto/ mark penny, 26-27 Getty Images/Clarissa Leahy